Alone, Alone, All, All Alone

ALONE, ALONE, ALL, ALL ALONE

David Belgum

PUBLISHING HOUSE

ST. LOUIS   LONDON

Concordia Publishing House, St. Louis, Missouri
Concordia Publishing House Ltd., London, E. C. 1
Copyright © 1972 Concordia Publishing House
ISBN 0-570-0674-2

CONTENTS

INTRODUCTION

A Parable About Change

Toward the end of the Middle Ages there once lived a serf who was attached to a feudal lord. In exchange for his faithful service he was given the privilege of living in a small hut just outside the castle wall. There he also had a small garden in which he could raise his own potatoes and turnips. There were both advantages and disadvantages for this humble servant who had descended from several generations of serfs in the village. In fact he knew no other kind of life.

On the one hand, it was a peaceful scene with the cattle in the meadow and the chapel bell ordering the day from sunrise to sunset. There was also security for him and his family in troubled times, because hostile bands of Vikings and other enemies were kept at bay by the lord's knights. At any sign of danger a bell rang and the drawbridge thundered with the hoofs of the nobleman's little mounted army. The serf and his family would scamper over the drawbridge before it was raised and find safety within the castle walls.

Some obvious disadvantages included lack of freedom, a meager diet, and few if any of the luxuries of life. There were few labor-saving devices, slight provisions for medical care, and educational opportunities were nil for the lowly peasant.

It so happened that the times were changing, and the serf's son found himself living in a rapidly growing and crowded town nearby in Flanders. How different things were for him working at his weaving loom among many other weavers. There was a constant effort to develop larger, faster, and more efficient looms. No longer could the worker count on his own little garden, but he had to go to the town market for his vegetables. There was no peaceful pastoral scene outside his hut's door, for now the serf's son looked across the street at another long row of crowded houses. No lord offered the protection of his castle, and it was every man for himself in the brawling town.

Now let us consider what attitude the serf's son should take toward the changing times. The die-hard approach would be to smash the looms, dismantle the town, and everyone head back for the good old days of the feudal lord, the little army of knights, the bell and drawbridge, and the hut with its own potato patch below the castle wall. Obviously this would not suffice because, as we know from our vantage point, the transition we have alluded to was nothing compared with the cotton gin, steam-driven knitting mills, and railroads that were to follow. What few feudal castles remain are either national shrines, interesting ruins, or converted tourist accommodations.

Another approach, and much more fruitful, would have been an effort to learn how to live in the new situation, to learn a way of surviving in the town and maybe even speculating on how to make town life better and more workable. The wife had better learn how to shop at the vegetable market and adapt menus to what is available. Those who could not adapt to the new rhythm of work, the new social structures, and the new life-style would have a rougher time of it than those who were oriented toward the future and committed to its development.

So it is with the contemporary migrants from farms, towns, and personalized groupings when they move into megalopolis or into one of the vast industrial complexes, governmental bureaucracies, or educational institutions. The question before modern man at the end of the 20th century is: Should he try to re-create the intimacy of personalized society, or should he adjust to new patterns of social organization and a new life-style?

> God grant me the serenity
> to accept the things I cannot change,
> the courage to change the things I can,
> and the wisdom to know the difference.

> (Alcoholics Anonymous)

PART I

WHY AM I
ALONE IN THE CROWD?

Crowding and overpopulation have attracted a lot of attention lately. Crowded superhighways and traffic-clogged cities; crowded apartment complexes in the big city and crowded school buses headed for big, consolidated schools in the rural towns; crowded campsites in the national parks to which millions are rushing trying to get away from the crowds back home.

Nowadays one gets the feeling that this would be a far better world if only half of us had been born. What a blessing if New York had only 5 million and Chicago only 2; if China and India had only a half or a third of their people. A revolutionary thought, and unthinkable 50 or 100 years ago. Until then we had believed the birth of every child was a welcome event much like we read in Ps. 127:3-5:

> Lo, sons are a heritage from the Lord,
>   the fruit of the womb a reward.
>
> Like arrows in the hand of a warrior
>   are the sons of one's youth.
>
> Happy is the man who has
>   his quiver full of them!

Population control is the watchword of the prophets of worldwide famine and doom. Pollution of every kind is blamed on the masses of people crowded upon our planet and exhausting its resources. Could this be one of the reasons for our loneliness and meaninglessness when we feel at times we are lost in the swirling crowd? Let us consider some significance of our mass society for us as persons.

CHAPTER 1

It Is a Depersonalized Society

The very nature of crowds is that they are not personal; call them depersonalized, suprapersonal, impersonal, or what you will.

Consider the crowded airport. The only thing that draws them together is that they are all leaving town via some airline: some for Cleveland, others for Atlanta, Wichita, New York, or Los Angeles — in random groups of 30, 60, or 150. It is completely incidental that one is going to a sales meeting, another to his father's funeral, and a third to get married. The main thing these human beings have in common as far as the crowded air terminal is concerned is that they all have to funnel through these ticket lines and corridors as a means of getting to their destination.

The same is true of a crowded department store or large cafeteria, the elevators in a tall office building, parking lots, the state fair, concert halls, waiting rooms of hospitals, etc. Each person has his own reason for being there, which may range from joy to sorrow, from economic necessity to leisure, from love to hate, from anxiety to peace of mind. The individuals have personal characteristics of age, sex, height, weight, intelligence, beliefs, etc., which are unique to each one; but those are not the factors that bring them together if they are in a true crowd. There is one suprapersonal factor that draws them to this place: food for their lunch hour, a post-Christmas white sale on bed linens, the need to find a parking place, sickness, or a highly adver-tised movie for their entertainment.

The Case of the "Depersonalized" Co-ed

Take a large Midwestern university women's dormitory as an example of depersonalized society. In the cafeteria the basic concern of the architect, the cook, the head of that particular residence hall is this: How in the world can we get 1,600 women in-fed-and-out-again during a rather brief lunch hour? Oh, it would be nice to have a pleasing decor, relaxed atmosphere, and chance for socializing during the hurried lunch hour; but let's face it, this is no family breakfast nook. This is institutionalized living. The solution was simple. Divide the cafeteria in half so that there will be two lines with only 800 in each line.

Now it so happened that a freshman from a small town was in line A because her student registration number (odd vs. even or some other arbitrary classification) was 20-3545-82 (her Social Security number). Meanwhile, the only other friends from her home town (two in number) had student numbers that put them in line B. She came to a counselor full of homesickness and loneliness. What could be done? She could drop out and go home to familiar surroundings; the dean of women could intervene and require the food service supervisor to reassign the lonely one so that all three friends could be in line B; or the little freshman could learn how to make friends in line A for lunch and meet her old friends at other times.

The most obvious solution and the most humane would seem to be some effort to rehumanize this mob scene. After all, were persons made for the cafeteria, or was the cafe-teria made for persons (to paraphrase Jesus' remark about the Sabbath)? Another way to approach the problem might be the larger and more general question of how to help this young woman adjust and adapt to the depersonalized social structures she may have to live with the next 40 or 50 years. For example, if she finishes her home economics course in fabrics, she may find herself eating in a large cafeteria at General Motors not too unlike the one at the big, depersonalized university; or if she finishes her nursing course, she could just as likely as not be working in some large hospital. In either case the cashier may be more interested in the number on her plastic charge plate certifying that she is indeed an employee than in her name and home town.

By the way, when this same student goes to the registrar's office to check on her course transcript, she may introduce herself by name to the clerk at the counter; but nothing will happen until she answers the little question, "What is your student ID (identification) number?" Once that number is punched on the computer or the large automated file machine, the answer will be forthcoming quick as a wink. But what did she want: a friendly visit, or her transcript sent out in the afternoon mail?

The same depersonalization process operates whenever a person is classified or presents himself in a given category: patron at a bank, customer in a department store, patient in a hospital, user of the telephone system, member of a labor union, subscriber to a national magazine, client of the welfare system, draftee in the army, etc., ad infinitum. Whenever you are part of a crowd, part of the mass, you can expect a certain amount of depersonalization. It is a fact of life whether essential, inevitable, for better or for worse; that is just the way it seems to be and is becoming increasingly more so.

The question is, "What attitude shall we take toward this trend in social organization?" Harking back to our "parable of change," we can learn how to live in the new situation or hanker for the "good old days" of the feudal lord, the little army of knights, the bell and drawbridge, and the hut with its own potato patch below the castle wall.

I am personally having some difficulty making this transition as exemplified by adjusting to the changes in the telephone procedures. It used to be that you simply dialed "0" for your helpful telephone operator, gave her an assignment, and she helped you "make the connection." There would be little exchanges like, "Do you want me to try later?" or, "I think the line is busy, but let me try again." There was a lot of "Please" and "Thank you." The other day I wanted to phone a chaplain in another hospital and dialed "0" for operator after dialing "9" to get "outside" of our own hospital. Rather than do the work for me like in the "good old days," she informed me that I could get his number by dialing the Universal Information operator (1-515-555-1212). Fine, after getting the number, I had to dial 157 (our intrastate interinstitutional line) plus long distance (1), his area code and number. In short, I spun the dial 25 times under the new system. I know it is here to stay, and maybe will become more complex; I know intellectually that it makes sense to do this work by electronic machine; but I am the first to admit it is somewhat of an adjustment. Every now and then Huxley's *Brave New World* or Orwell's *1984* looms up over the horizon, and there is the stubborn impulse to say, "No! I refuse to move on down the line into this depersonalized kind of society."

Being Unique Is Something Else

There are times when you are not just another person in the line, in the crowd. Those are the times when no one can take your place, when you are an individual who cannot be replaced. You are an only son or a mother, a father or fiancé regardless of whether your Interbank credit card treats you like just one among many computerized customers to be run through the electronic accounting machine. As an individual you have your own, very personal feelings about sunsets, stamp collecting, Wagnerian opera, family picnics, your clubfoot or bald head. It is certain that no other person in the crowded traffic lanes has the same identical combination of feelings and attitudes about the above assortment of experiences any more than anyone else has your set of fingerprints.

One of the great fears of our age is that some steam-roller process of depersonalization will turn us into automatons, robots, store-window mannequins created by mass production and informed by the mass media. Instead of being allowed to flower in individual shades and design, we will be pressured by demands for conformity. It is this monotonous sameness that many dread when they think of depersonalization. The uniformity of militarism with its lockstep march, the long lines of prisoners in concentration camps (sloppily dressed in dull rags but with an identification number neatly tatooed on each body), and the servile obedience to totalitarian demands, the individual sacrificed for the sake of some abstract entity called "The State"—these are the bad parts of depersonalization.

High religion calls us to preserve our own integrity in the face of external demands. As St. Paul wrote:

> Do not be conformed to this world, but be transformed by the renewal of your mind, that you may prove what is the will of God, what is good and acceptable and perfect.   (Rom. 12:2)

"And the Wisdom to Know the Difference"

The question each of us must answer is this: When is it appropriate to be counted as one among many in the crowd (in the airport), and when must we stand up and be counted as one against many (in taking a stand against some social injustice even when it is unpopular to do so)?

There has been much misplaced and inappropriate

17

anger directed at technology, statistical record keeping, efficiency-motivated processes, etc. Pious complaints against machinery assume that the "sin" lies in the device man has made. Hardly! The wheel, the knife, printing presses, and rope are neither sinful nor righteous in themselves. The good or evil lies in the intention of the man using them. Wheels can roll me and my family out to the state park for a beautiful Sunday outing in God's outdoor playground, or, of course, I can use wheels for a rapid getaway from a bank robbery. The knife can be used for murder or life-giving open-heart surgery. On the same press we can print lies and pornography and propaganda, or melt down the lead slugs and reset the type for printing the Sermon on the Mount. With a rope we can lynch a neighbor or pull him out of a crevice into which he has slipped while hiking in the mountains.

Let us not complain and lament about depersonalization of things that do not count, aspects of our lives that can just as well be quantified and measured in mass terms. In urban and industrial societies there are many facts about the populace which simply must be tabulated in order to provide necessary services of health, education, welfare, transportation, housing, municipal services, urban and regional planning of water and sewer systems, manpower utilization for maximum employment, and others. It is quite proper to be treated impersonally for the sake of such broad surveys and large-scale enterprises. Governmental surveys, consumer statistics, sociological analysis, and other approaches to the needs of mankind in the mass can be a great blessing to millions if wholesome services are brought to bear responsively upon human needs. As Joseph Sitler said once in a speech, to bring a cup of cold water in Jesus' name in Chicago may require floating a $20 million bond issue to finance an expansion of the city waterworks. In that case the most water is delivered to the greatest number precisely by not being very personal about it.

On the other hand, each person must have such a keen sense of his own identity that he is not *only* a number, not *only* a statistic in the U. S. Census Report. Each of us must preserve our freedom to make our own decisions, to accept or reject the advertising thrust upon us, to express our honest conviction even when to do so leaves us standing alone—alone when we would rather be part of the crowd. Yes, we must ask ourselves if there are not reasons for which to die rather than to forsake our integrity. St. Stephen was alone in a crowd; but for a time Peter was not able to be alone and denied his Lord so that he would be thought part of the crowd. Consider Jesus in the Garden of Gethsemane.

A child of God knows when to be in communion with the crowd and when to be alone.

CHAPTER 2

Other People Do Not Help Me

Communication is not easy in our complicated society. But how can others help us unless we tell them clearly what we need? Do you have pain in your side? A surgeon cannot help you unless you are willing to present yourself to the clinic, fill out the application form, answer the examining doctor's questions, etc. "Oh," you say, "you mean others cannot provide me with useful answers if they do not know my questions." Often today such communication is made through standardized, prearranged methods. Unless requests are directed to the right place and through the right channels, there is no way of "plugging into the circuit." Too complicated? Maybe so, but realistically speaking that's the name of the game these days.

Reference shelves in libraries hold many directories listing agencies and resources, in short, where to go for help. Once you know the combination to the lock, you can open up a whole list of groups and persons highly trained and sincerely motivated to help exactly you and help you perhaps better than your dearest friend. The resources are as wide-ranging as human need — from blindness to old age assistance, from unmarried parenthood to employment opportunities, from road conditions in your favorite vacation area to help for your mentally retarded son. Some social service agencies spend almost all their time just putting persons with problems in touch with sources of help. The help may be psychiatric, financial, religious, legal, social, physical, environmental, recreational, to name only a few types.

Even a recent social invention to help break through red tape in government, such as the "ombudsman," can make only a small dent in the system. One such public servant has been appointed by the governor in my state. This respected public servant is supposed to help stray, confused citizens who cannot find their way through the intricacies of the tax bureau, the state welfare department, laws protecting tenants in civil rights suits, and others. It is nevertheless expected that the vast majority of people will find their way through the maze by themselves; otherwise the nice personal office of ombudsman will itself become a vast bureau trying to handle the individual needs of 3 million citizens.

So if you raise the plaintive cry, "Other people do not help me," perhaps part of the problem is that you do not, cannot, or do not know how to ask for help. Let us break down the helping enterprise into its several parts. In short, what do you have to do in order to *let* others help you?

Knowing personally what you need may seem obvious and simple, but it is not. The ancient philosopher admonished, "Know thyself." We are more willing to know good things about ourselves than bad. Sometimes we have developed such a pattern of self deception that we do not know some very important things about ourselves. We become unable to acknowledge honestly and objectively the fact, which is plain enough to others, that we are: an alcoholic, about to lose our job, in the midst of a sick marriage, on the brink of a nervous breakdown, or that we will lose the family farm. All these sad things make us feel inadequate; there is a stigma attached to them. It is less painful to put such "facts" out of our mind. Now if we have repressed them out of our own consciousness, obviously we become not very available for receiving help from others, from personal friends and family or from a large institutionalized agency.

One way to get to know ourselves better is to practice honesty in all our dealings, convinced that our hurt pride is not nearly as serious in the long run as the doom toward which we are headed by following a blind path of least resistance. Hardly any of these troubles just go away or get better by themselves, especially if we are hiding our heads in the sand like an ostrich.

Telling openly lets others know what is going on inside us, in our personal lives. It is confession, the opposite of hypocrisy. Yet it is amazing how many of us basically distrust openness. We believe that pretending things are all right when they are not will somehow pay off. Meanwhile the clandestine affair gets more complicated, the malignant tumor gets larger, we fall deeper and deeper into debt or farther behind in schoolwork. Often the result is a sad fact: "If you had only told us about it sooner, we could have helped you" (by marriage counseling, surgery for the tumor, refinancing your mortgage, or remedial tutoring or rearrangement of your course schedule).

Just as we mentioned in the first chapter that there is a general fear of the machine, so in regard to institutional record keeping there is a fear of having oneself known publicly. If I go for help to _____ agency, my case will go on record and I may be publicly known for who I am: an alcoholic, an unemployment case, a welfare client, perhaps a former mental hospital patient. I would rather be known as the big, strong, self-made American or the normal, healthy, successful person. If I do not tell others I need help, my name will never be "on the blotter"; I will not be known by others as I know myself to be.

In reply to a plea on the part of a prominent person that if he were known as a person having a given problem he might lose his job, the words of Jesus rang clear:

For what will it profit a man if he gains the whole world and forfeits his life?   (Matt. 16:26)

Listening carefully to the experience, advice, and suggestions of others is so precarious a stance for troubled people that most counselors are cautioned not even to try advice-giving. It is so humiliating to be dependent on another that the following is not an uncommon outburst: "I don't have to take that from you." You see, if I "have to take that from you," it means that I am in a dependent, receiving position. Patients have gone from one doctor to another to be rediagnosed, but have repeatedly not "heard" the physician's explanations. One of the serious contributors to loneliness is the refusal to receive from others. True fellowship and a sense of community is the combination of give-and-take. Once we have made the big step of *telling openly,* we must take the reciprocal step of listening carefully.

Doing willingly whatever it takes to get back on the track may sound easy; but talk is sometimes cheap and action comes hard. Consider the complaint expressed in the heading of this chapter: "Other people do not help me." The way the problem is stated is part of the problem. No matter how much compassion, understanding empathetic listening, and helping others do for and to me, there comes a time when I must *do* for myself, accept responsibility for my own actions. Frequently such proposed action has been talked about at the counselor's office, at the bank, in church, in the group therapy session in the mental health center, and among friends. The acid test now comes: Will I *do* those things which will create a new style of life, provide concrete progress toward a solution, make me a more mature and useful person in society?

Naaman is a case in point. He was a proud Syrian military commander, but had leprosy. He had great expectations of being healed by the prophet Elisha. He had gone

23

through the first three steps above, but balked at what he was asked to do—a simple little thing like washing in the river Jordan. Fortunately, just before he was ready to leave in disgust, one of his servants put it to him this way:

My father, if the prophet had commanded you to do some great thing, would you not have done it? How much rather, then, when he says to you, "Wash and be clean?" (2 Kings 5:13)

Yes, near the end of your wrestling with this question you do well to change the focus of attention from others to self when it comes to the doing. Translate a new attitude and new sharing into new action.

A concluding thought brings us back to the start of this chapter, a reference to how best to hook up with the helping systems available in our society.

In most instances the fastest and most accurate route to help is through channels prescribed for that purpose. Go to the supply window without your requisition form, and how is the agent supposed to know you are entitled to those supplies? Go to the hearing clinic without your folder and case record from the otolaryngologist, and how will the technician know which tests you need? Go to the employment counselor without your aptitude scores, previous work record, and other identifications, and it will just take him twice as long to get acquainted with your "case."

A hang-up for some people is that they assume that as soon as they ask for help, they will become "depersonalized," they will be thought of as a "case" and run through some complicated procedures. But some of that is inevitable. Unless one is willing to "classify" himself, put himself in a "category," he will not receive the help that is available in that specialized place in the community whether it be the fire station, police station, hospital, family service agency, vocational rehabilitation center, or what have you.

If you want help in our day and age, you have to use today's methods, and not those of the serf in the "good old days" of the feudal lord, the little army of knights, the bell and drawbridge, and the hut with its own potato patch below the castle wall.

CHAPTER 3

I Lack Precisely What I Need Most

> I tell you that to every one who has
> will more be given; but from him who has not,
> even what he has will be taken away.
>
> (Luke 19:26)

How true the above motto seems in everyday life. The rich man, who can afford to pay interest, is able to pay cash and maybe even get a discount through his business connections. The poor man, who can least afford it, must pay high interest rates and is most likely to be victimized by a loan shark. The one who most needs a break is surely the least capable, least popular, least well-adjusted person; yet he or she is precisely the one who is not offered the job, not invited to the party, seldom paid a compliment.

Today there is a growing rejection of poverty and a deeper sympathy for the suffering of the "have-nots," the underdeveloped nations, the handicapped, and disadvantaged. Much of such a compassionate attitude also stems from the Gospel of love for fellowman. What are we to make of the above words of Jesus where He implies that the natural course of events will be for the poor to get poorer and the fortunate to become more fortunate?

The crippled, paralyzed, or amputated patient in the rehabilitation ward comes to mind in connection with the above text. A critical question in his recovery is this: Does he focus on what he still has left, or does he concentrate on what he "has not," his disabling condition? The patient who turns most of his attention to what is missing is tempted toward self-pity, cynicism, and a pessimistic retreat from the future. The one who begins to ask if it is possible to learn to type with one hand, to ask when he could start a series of tests to find what other vocations are open to him which he could perform adequately from a wheelchair, or if he is eligible for the "talking book" program, etc., that person is the one about whom the staff gets enthusiastic; he has a far greater chance because unto him "will be given." It is interesting that when Jesus confronts the paralytic by the pool of healing, who had lain there in that health spa 38 years, He begins by asking him straight out, "Do you want to be healed?" A good question according to any hospital chaplain acquainted with patients who actually do not wish to be healed.

Unfortunately the patient with "hospitalitis" has found his sick role, his dependent situation, more rewarding than normal life. In his weakened condition he is not responsible for meeting his sales quota, getting to work on time, facing up to mistakes on the job or tension in the family. There are people whose lot in life is so disastrous that sickness is an acceptable price to pay for the privilege of "getting away from it all." There are other ways of "copping out" of course—alcohol, drugs, daydreaming. Such persons say, and understandably so, "What have I got to lose?" The sad and seemingly unjust reality is this: "Yes, you don't have much now, but in your case things will get even worse."

Determinism vs. Freedom of Choice

Philosophers have argued both sides of the question: "Is man's life determined by forces beyond his control, or is he free to choose his own life-style and follow it?" In layman's terms it goes like this. "I guess my number was up." "That bullet didn't have my name on it." "What can I do; *everything's* against me!" Some blame their lot on God, some on "the system," others on nature or forces of "fate." Heredity, social conditioning, early learning experiences, parental influence, limitations of personal capacity, lack of opportunity—these are various ways of saying, "I'm stuck with a bad situation not of my own making, and there is nothing I can do about it."

Psychologists have also wrestled with this question. But how do you prove in the final analysis that man has or does not have the freedom of choice he might like to think he has? It is pretty difficult to run man through the same experience twice in a scientific manner, because the second time some learning may have benefited him. To show how futile the argument can get, the following standoff is instructive as well as slightly humorous.

A believer in behaviorism and determinism tried in his inimitable and reductionistic way to undercut his friend's line of reasoning by saying, "You just think that way because of your early childhood experiences." To which the reply in kind was, "You just say I think that way because of my early childhood experiences because of your childhood experiences." Obviously there was no point in even discussing it further, because they would go around in endless circles, each undercutting the other.

Who or What Will Break the Tie?

Instead of continuing the endless debate, let us shift the center of attention from the age-old question to the person in the middle of the dilemma and ask what his attitude is. What does he believe about his situation? Maybe for all practical purposes if he says he is trapped, he is trapped. At least if he believes his situation is hopeless, that very belief becomes a significant part of the total situation. Another belief, that he really has several possible alternatives which are worth trying, would increase his *sense* of freedom, and in fact his real freedom to act. There is a little phrase, which may be taken out of context, but it still gives a challenge at this point: "For as he thinketh in his heart, so is he." (Prov. 23:7 KJV)

Remember how impossible the disciples thought it was to heal the son with a dumb spirit. No wonder! It had complete control over the young man. The father said: "Wherever it seizes him, it dashes him down; and he foams and grinds his teeth and becomes rigid . . . . And it has often cast him into the fire and into the water to destroy him; but if You can do anything, have pity on us and help us." And Jesus said to him, "If you can! All things are possible to him who believes." To which the father replied, "I believe; help my unbelief!" When the disciples asked why they could not heal the poor demoniac, Jesus replied, "This kind cannot be driven out by anything but prayer" (Mark 9:14-29). Surely not by sitting around convinced that everything is fatalistically locked into place. Like the song goes, "What will be will be."

What saved the young man? Was it not faith? Note the father's plea: "I believe; help my unbelief!" To the unsuccessful disciples Jesus had said, "O faithless generation!" Even at that the help came from Jesus as an act of grace, which leads us to our next point.

Grace: The Unique Variable

The trouble with searching out only the determining conditions and the conditioning determinants in a mechanistic way is that there is much more to *human* life than that. We must not jump too quickly from the experiments in the rat cage and mazes to the fully human life situation. Grace is the surprising variable in the human experiment. When man thinks he has taken all else into account, there yet remains the uncontrolled variable of the *grace* of God.

Nicodemus was a highly educated and intelligent man who got hung up on this very point, that he could not *understand* intellectually the change that comes over a man when he is "born anew . . . of water and the Spirit" (a work of grace). Jesus continued to explain the mystery. "The wind blows where it wills, and you hear the sound of it, but you do not know whence it comes or whither it goes; so it is with every one who is born of the Spirit" (John 3:1-15). The person committed to God does not limit his life or expectations to those things he can nail down, prove, demonstrate or trace to his fatalistic conditionings. In some strange way he is free as the wind.

Yes, you quite rightly say, "I lack precisely what I need most." Because grace, what you need most, is *given* from above.

Does acknowledging grace through faith make a person dependent in a kind of inactive, pitifully helpless sense? Not at all. Such a one rather feels himself in tune with the source of all power, God his Creator and Sustainer. Such a one is not alone, for "underneath are the everlasting arms." He is motivated by gratitude and joy to use all his energies and to be a good steward of whatever the Lord has entrusted to him, even if it is only one pound or talent (see Luke 19:11-27), one foot or one eye, a small retarded intelligence or a low social standing.

Maybe it takes more grace to use a little capacity. The big genius will always find a way; the clever businessman will be able to rebuild his fortune if it is temporarily lost; the healthy and popular have little difficulty making it in society. In fact the aforementioned are sorely tempted to claim all the credit for their successes and stumble on the sin of successful people, that is, PRIDE. Let us close with another word from the Gospel set over against the one at the head of this chapter. It is from the beautiful and inspiring Magnificat of Mary:

He has shown strength with His arm,
He has scattered the proud in the
imagination of their hearts,
He has put down the mighty from their thrones,
and exalted those of low degree;
He has filled the hungry with good things,
and the rich He has sent empty away.

(Luke 1:51-53)

PART II

HOW WAS IT
IN THE OLDEN DAYS?

Even when my kids don't ask me, I like to tell them "how it was in the olden days." It is pleasant to romanticize about the past, especially on days when things are a bit grim, when it's been a while since our last success, or when present-day expectations seem unreasonable.

Ah! I can remember what a pleasant experience it was to sit with my father in the hay mow of the barn looking out on the green pasture and willow-lined creek and listening to a spring rain patter on the shingles. There was security, fellowship, acceptance, and some stories of Norse gods or the classic Greek myths (which represented in their turn "the olden days").

We all know the experience of reverie and fantasy as fairly harmless escape from reality if it does not last too long and interfere with our daily work or social relationships. But sometimes we cast longing eyes back on the good old days in ways that are not very helpful. We make unfortunate comparisons taking the best of those days and the worst of our own time. No wonder the present or future does not come off very well.

Since we spent some time in Part I considering the present and future *depersonalized* society, it is only fair to review some forgotten aspects of the *personalized* way of life. Since you can be trusted to remember all the good points, you will pardon me for bringing to remembrance the less favorable side.

CHAPTER 4

Life in a Personalized Society

Was it all so wonderful? Some of our more serious ethical problems stemmed from very close personal connections, the use of personal influence and connections when a more objective approach was called for. Consider a few of these.

Simony was the attempt to obtain special favor, such as appointment to an ecclesiastical office in the church through an exchange of gifts, often money. Simon Magus tried to buy his way into the rank of apostle in New Testament times. In effect it is saying, "You and I can make a personal, private deal that the rest of them don't have to know about." Very personal, very cozy, but not nice.

Nepotism comes from the Latin word for nephew. Giving one's nephew preferential treatment in business or politics is about as personal as you can get — too personal, as a matter of fact, especially if he is not qualified for the job. The same goes for cousins, college roommates, sons-in-law, pals from boyhood days, etc. Many a New England knitting mill went bankrupt because the reins of management were handed down to relatives with little regard for their qualifications as superintendents, plant managers, or vice-presidents. Other companies have suffered through the "I have a friend who can get it for you wholesale" practice. This approach sometimes backfires when the next customer complains, "What's so special about him? I've had dealings with this firm longer than he — it's not fair!"

Bribery or graft is likewise a shortcut, receiving the contract for some municipal project through personal and special connection instead of through the official letting of bids, which is public and above board. Bribery does not need to involve millions of dollars of state or federal money. It can be as simple as not giving a parking ticket to my landlord for fear he will do me dirt in return for his well-deserved ticket. There are the numerous situations in which appeal is made to personal relationship. "You wouldn't do that to your old buddy, would you?" This implies that it would have been all right to have given the parking ticket to a stranger or a person who is so socially inept that he has neither friends nor connections. Sometimes the ethics sinks still lower when someone pleads in such a case, "What are friends for?" For cheating, I guess.

In business and professional circles it is sometimes very difficult to separate personal and official relationships. One shipping clerk had for years used a certain trucking firm to transport bulk paper from a Maine mill to Boston, as he told me, "because they're real nice people. . . . Every year they give me this desk calendar" (a vinyl novelty worth anywhere from $2.50 to $3.75). A new alert cost accountant just out of college computed the difference when the material, for which speed was not a factor, was shipped by rail—$17,000 a year. It was clearly the most expensive calendar in Boston.

How large does a personal favor in business have to be before it is unethical? A lunch and two drinks, tickets for the whole family to a professional football game, or an all-expense-paid week at Miami Beach at the height of the season? A *personal* favor, at least.

Qualifications (with a footnote on how to avoid the pitfalls of the "Peter principle")

It is hard to say no to persons with whom you have

a nice personal relationship. This is especially true for any person who wants to be known as a "nice guy." Couple with this the temptation of the American dream of progress, upward mobility, promotions, and the general motto of EXCELSIOR. One can almost hear the trumpets blazing away as the ideal American goes from one rung to the other up the ladder of success. (I must hasten to add that one definition of "excelsior" is "a material of curled shreds of wood used for stuffing upholstery.")

The Peter principle describes persons whose shirts have been prematurely stuffed with status and dignity. They have risen to the "level of their *in*competence." In other words, they did not know where to stop, were not content with what they could do well. Thus many a president of a college should have remained dean, and the dean might have been better off as a competent professor, and so on down the line. One remedy for this unfortunate state of affairs might seem naively simple and so would be voted down in any organization; but give it your careful consideration.

Let each person use all the pull and connections he can muster, working fiendishly for promotions and success until he or she is 50 years old. Then let him or her step down one notch, and he will very likely be in his rightful place — at the level of his competence. So a 50-year-old bishop will step down from his high office and become pastor of one of the large parishes in his territory. The minister of the 2,000 member church will accept a call to one of 1,500, and so on down the line. Don't knock it till you've tried it; maybe you know someone who has.

Seriously, you have no doubt guessed that the solution to the problem is *qualifications*, not "connections" as in the personalized methods stated above: simony, nepotism, graft, or more subtle types. A young friend assured me that he was particularly pleased that he had obtained a fine position in the trust department of a large bank because of his aptitudes, capacity, and potential as represented by his law college credentials rather than getting the job through personal connections.

Yes, the personalized society of the olden days did have its built-in pitfalls, as is likely true of any type of society. What was done to deal with the problem of misplaced persons? Gradually, over the years, there developed more detailed and accurate record keeping. The public school instituted the "cumulative record" that followed the pupil from kindergarten through high school. Put such information together with the personnel officer's record at the plant where a young man has worked the past five years, and you have a pretty accurate estimate of his abilities and capacities to do certain tasks. If you wanted to know more about him, you could get his permission to examine the last physical examination report his physician compiled. Throw in some psychological tests for good measure, and it is amazing how much can be known about this person from such a compilation.

In a strange way all this record keeping has not depersonalized the young worker as much as it has brought out precisely his own unique characteristics. To whom do all these pieces and bits of information belong? To him, of course, and to no one else. In no one else will you find exactly this combination of factors, this pattern of characteristics, this sequence of diverse experiences. A look at his record convinces you that no other person is the duplicate of *this person.* As his fingerprint is uniquely his own, so is his record with its complex picture of who he is and what he has done.

If on top of all else a person has a mature openness and honest integrity, he is quite willing to have others in society know who he is, what he can do, and what his capacity is as he looks toward vocational placement. Add to this a desire to fit in, with a sense of Christian stewardship of his talents and energies, where the needs of society call him, and you have a man headed toward worthy work. He is not interested in sliding into a niche where he does not belong, where he will be a misfit, even if a friend or relative offered it to him as a "favor." Such a view of selfhood and vocation is one's best safeguard against simony, nepotism, bribery, and the pitfalls of the Peter Principle.

Status per se vs. Function per alia

Status *for its own sake* is an unseemly sight, and we have just begun to realize how status conscious we have been even in our supposedly democratic America. The more we understand about status seeking, the more pointless it becomes. It is so indirect and roundabout. Rather than buying a certain kind of car to show how worthy a person one is, let him buy an automobile for transportation, safety, comfort, etc., and then do something more dynamic to make his worth as a person secure. This is one reason for the generation gap. A young person will say about a clear status symbol, "Who needs it?" The young are saying, "Do it if it is useful, beautiful, helpful, but don't do it to *show off!*" "He bugs me, because he is *phony!*" "You know, I don't think she's for *real.*"

Function *for the sake of others,* service motivated, or in Luther's terms — to be a little Christ to one's neighbor. That's the name of the game. If I become principal of a school *in order to* coordinate the facilities, persons, and curriculum so that as many pupils as possible have a good learning experience, that is a worthy function. Any status, authority, respect, etc., which might further that end are just so many tools to get the job done. Such a person does not first say, "I want a job that will get me a little respect around here and some status in the community; maybe I'll try being a school principal, or better yet, the *superintendent.*" In that latter attitude, obviously the function he fulfills, the service he renders would be quite secondary.

Let us transfer these general principles into the specific field of health care. People used to seek out nice personal relationships with a family physician who knew their individual case and their family intimately. It was a warm personal relationship—for those who could afford it. Meanwhile, a large multitude got minimal delivery of health care. A careful study by Duff and Hollingshead, *Sickness and Society*, documents the fact that the very rich and the very poor got poor medical care—the rich because they could pull rank on the physician and call their own shots, and the poor for obvious reasons. How much better it would have been if each person were treated simply according to his or her medical need. In other words, you would receive treatment for your disordered gall bladder simply because it is diseased, not according to your socio-economic status, the length of residency in the state or county, and other nonmedical aspects of your personal identity.

> But a Samaritan, as he journeyed, came to where he was; and when he saw him, he had compassion, and went to him and bound up his wounds, pouring on oil and wine; then he set him on his own beast and brought him to an inn and took care of him.
> (Luke 10:33-34)

He did all this without knowing anything about his personal identity. He bound up his wounds simply because they were wounds, and he had compassion on his condition. He was concerned to fulfill this function *for the sake of others*. He was service conscious, not status conscious.

> You have heard that it was said, "You shall love your neighbor and hate your enemy." But I say to you,

Love your enemies and pray for those who persecute you, so that you may be sons of your Father who is in heaven; for He makes His sun rise on the evil and on the good, and sends rain on the just and on the unjust. For if you love those who love you, what reward have you? Do not even the tax collectors do the same? And if you salute only your brethren, what more are you doing than others?

(Matt. 5:43-47)

St. Peter discovered that it takes the grace of God to avoid being a respecter of persons.

You yourselves know how unlawful it is for a Jew to associate with or to visit anyone of another nation, but God has shown me that I should not call any man common or unclean. So when I was sent for, I came without objection. I ask then why you sent for me.

(Acts 10:28-29)

CHAPTER 5

Hester's "A," a Big Help?

Remember Nathaniel Hawthorne's story *The Scarlet Letter*? Hester Prynne committed adultery and was required by the community to wear a large red letter A to signify her moral defect. It was a kind of stigma that fulfilled several purposes. First there was the punishment for her sin. Maybe there was also the practical value of marking such a woman. In effect it was saying to all wives in the community, "When you see that Hester woman prowling around, better keep a close eye on your husband; she's just the kind who might snatch him away from you." Hester was not the first to bear a mark, nor the last.

The term "stigma" comes from a Greek word meaning "tattoo." It was convenient to make a mark or brand on slaves, criminals, also unfit citizens who were ostracized. That way one could tell at a glance that the person was not to be trusted, was unfit for public office in the city-state, ineligible to marry your daughter, unreliable in business transactions. It was a social kind of shorthand character reading at a glance—crude, maybe, but that is how it was then and, in a sense, is to this day.

Marking persons is a very old practice. We hear of the mark of Cain in Genesis. Circumcision was the mark signifying that a man belonged to the chosen people of Israel. Labels can be good or bad; but in a very real sense, once you are marked or labeled, it sticks to you like a tattoo, like a stigma.

Two Modern Hesters
Two Ways of Handling Stigma

Two young women belonged to the same rather strict congregation in rural Iowa. It was a tightly knit ethnic community where everyone knew everyone else very intimately. They both became pregnant while still single, but there the similarity stopped. The one took off for Seattle because she was sure the "church people" would judge her harshly; she could only find hope in a new life among strangers. The other used the method prescribed by the group: repentant confession before the congregation at Wednesday night prayer meeting. The latter found acceptance, forgiveness, and a new life right there at home and is now teaching Sunday school. The one who more or less tried to run away from her problem still suffers from anxiety, guilt, and a feeling of estrangement.

One lesson to be learned from the above comparison is that the most constructive approach to stigma is not to try to avoid it, but to face it and resolve it. Whether the problem is unmarried parenthood, mental retardation, a clubfoot, stuttering, harelip, alcoholism, amputation, minority group membership, obesity, or something else — anything you might name which you would classify as a handicap to you, something you might wish were otherwise, something causing you distress — the answer to the problem is not to run away and hide in some anonymity, not to get lost in the crowd, or to pretend it is not a problem. Unless you have dealt with your problem and come to grips with it, it may not be solved by a change in geography.

The Town Clown
The Other Side of the Coin

In the "olden days" problems cases were handled rather informally in the personalized society. An eccentric old grandmother was tolerated quite well out on the farm feeding *and* talking to chickens. Maybe she stayed in the back room when company came to the big farm house. In a big city her senility would be so conspicuous and bothersome that she would be sent to a mental hospital or some other "home" for care. The town drunk or village idiot was likewise tolerated with condescending remarks such as: "Oh, don't pay any attention to old Jake; he just *is* like that." "You can't expect too much from _____, you know; he's kind'a odd." Or, as if summing up a long social service case history in capsule form, "The Heilingdoerfers have *always* been *that way.*"

In one sense it was a bit like the serf in his little hut beside the castle wall in that he knew his place, and his lot in life was not expected to change. In one sense, when you have been labelled "the town drunk" often enough, you come to look upon it as a job description—this is how I am expected to act, so I had better do what is expected of me. In that sense the stigma, the label, the clear and ever-present identity did not help a person to change. One sank deeper and deeper into his routine, his role, his rut. It was often hard to get a new start. In other words, Hester's "A" is not always a big help.

Not everyone got a new start like the young woman mentioned above who overcame her problem right there in her own little rural community. But remember, she made use of the redemptive resource of the congregation. That same resource was available to the girl who took off for Seattle, too, but for some reason she did not trust it, did not make use of it, or something got in the way.

A New Start in a New Place

The Lord said to Abram, "Go from your country and your kindred and your father's house to the land that I will show you" (Gen. 12:1). Take another case of leaving the familiar and making a new start in life: "Therefore a man leaves his father and his mother and cleaves to his wife, and they become one flesh" (Gen. 2:24). We worry about a child who cannot grow up and leave home, strike out on his own, cut the apron strings. Wise parents are pleased if their little boy can adjust to a week at Scout camp or church camp without undue homesickness.

My own experience is a case in point. I grew up in a Norwegian Lutheran community in Minnesota. Wherever I turned someone was identifying me with someone or another: father, uncles, brothers, cousins. When I was ordained, the clan effect was intensified. The following relatives were also pastors: my father, brother, two uncles, and six cousins, plus a brother in Lutheran social service who traveled widely. Add to this a bevy of in-laws, nieces, sister, and other relatives who had attended nearby church colleges, and the plot thickened.

When I accepted a call to a parish in Boston, I suddenly realized how glad I was to be known simply for myself. Obviously in that city of Irish Catholics, Yankee Congregationalists and Methodists, Unitarians, and Christian Scientists I'd have to make it on my own and not by the associations with and good name of the numerous namesakes and relatives listed above. This was true even though I got along fine with all those good folks and appreciated them in many ways. But it was nice being able to make it all alone out there in the new world.

Let us repeat the warning: If a new start in a new place is escape from responsibility, avoidance of confrontation, a substitute for resolving a problem, don't expect it to be a blessing, a new covenant like for Abraham. But there can be opportunity for new growth in maturity, an objective testing of one's potential, a legitimate "second chance," etc., in a new situation.

In our depersonalized, mobile society (the average American now moves at least once every four years) there are many opportunities to try new life-styles, new settings, new relationships, new vocations. Perhaps life in a Chicago suburb suits you better than the one you now lead in Lone Tree, Iowa; try it. On the other hand, in five years you may be just as clear that you want to move back to a town and country style of life. Sure, it is less secure to experiment, but at least you may have the choice, which is more than can be said about the serf in the little hut beside the castle wall with the bell and drawbridge and potato patch. Of course the affluent have more choice and can afford to move about more freely than those in the ghetto.

On second thought, maybe you should review Chapters 1 and 4 before making any big changes. Weigh the advantages and disadvantages of the so-called depersonalized society; weigh in your mind the benefits and problems associated with a personalized life-style, if you still have it; then you make the decision. You be the judge. After all, it's your life.

CHAPTER 6

Skeleton on the Outside or Inside?

Crustacean animals, like lobsters, crabs, and oysters, have the boney or stiff means of support on the outside. Vertebrates, like man, have the skeleton on the inside. In this chapter we are concerned with the moral aspects of contemporary life. The analogy hinted at in the title is found in common speech. "He has no backbone" means he is lacking in moral capacity. Likewise, the "spineless" person "Stand up and take it like a man" means face up to your responsibility. "Don't be a jellyfish." Consider John the Baptist, whether he had his moral skeleton on the outside or inside according to Jesus' description:

> What did you go out into the wilderness to behold? A reed shaken by the wind? What then did you go out to see? A man clothed in soft raiment? Behold, those who are gorgeously appareled and live in luxury are in kings' courts. What then did you go out to see? A prophet? Yes, I tell you, and more than a prophet. . . . I tell you, among those born of women none is greater than John; yet he who is least in the kingdom of God is greater than he.
>
> (Luke 7:24-28)

Recalling the case of the "depersonalized" co-ed in Chapter 1, and remembering how lonely and unsupported she felt in the vast cafeteria at the dormitory, let us consider the challenges and adjustments required of her in the sphere of morality. Back home among family, friends, and neighbors she had many superegos looking over her shoulder.

For many of us good behavior is prompted by the desire to have loved ones and significant others think well of us. As children we want the approval of meaningful authority figures, the acceptance of our playmates; and in exchange for this we are willing to "do right." That is the *must* conscience of childhood. Hopefully, as we mature into adulthood, we will internalize a sense of morality and the capacity to make ethical decisions. This may be called the *ought* conscience of the responsible adult member of society. It is the transition from legalism to grace, from a life-style of compulsive obedience to one of loving service. Obviously most of us have difficulty attaining this higher and more spontaneous kind of moral life. (We're less likely to cheat on a parking meter when the meter maid strolls by.) But we can recognize it as a positive ideal. On occasions when we have operated on this higher level of love and grace, we have experienced a kind of joy that was not present when we were being forced by whiplash to "do right."

So what about our young co-ed after she graduates and moves into a 30th-floor apartment in a new environment? As we say, "She's on her own." Most of her external moral supports are left behind in her home town. All the ethics she has to guide her now is what she brings along in her own conscience — like her two suitcases and a hat box. Will she live on a lower moral level and have lower standards? Hardly, but now whatever level she lives on will more likely be her own. She is more likely to act her real self according to what she believes down deep is right or wrong, wasteful or useful, selfish or concerned for others.

It is quite a different ball game, making decisions where you are known and your reputation is clearly at stake or making ethical decisions where you suspect "it doesn't really matter because no one will *know*." Of course, one does not escape his conscience and moral background by getting on the Greyhound bus and kissing one's mother good-bye, or by moving one's family via Allied Van Lines to a new community to get away from the in-laws. Many a migraine headache, ulcer, anxiety attack, or profound depression is simply a reminder that the "rules of the game" are still the same. We were just temporarily deceived by our newfound freedom in the depersonalized society.

The point of the above discussion is that life in a more mobile, fast-paced, even depersonalized society separates the men from the boys as far as character is concerned. It becomes clear who has his moral and spiritual skeleton on the outside and who has it on the inside. Who can be counted on when some of the external supports are gone, when personal connections are severed through death, transfer, or just through changing conditions? Many do not handle their money, sexuality, language, etc., the same at the family reunion as they do at the American Legion convention, not the same around their home neighborhood as on vacation at Atlantic City.

Fracture or Rupture
You're Still in Trouble

Remember, we are still talking about morality, the kind of behavior and relationships which help to hold society together and hold the individual together at the same time — preserve his integrity. Times may change, forms of government may change, socioeconomic patterns vary from age to age. Nevertheless, certain basic moral elements remain essential for the individual as well as for the community. When these are broken or violated, individuals disintegrate and society suffers disorder. Regardless of your personality type or life-style, whether you have a strong skeleton or are a clam or a flabby jellyfish, immorality leads to brokenness. It is also at the center of much loneliness. The dictionary defines two kinds of brokenness: "Fracture commonly applies to hard, rupture to soft objects."

The external appearance of the new depersonalized society gives the impression that a new approach to ethics is called for. Hence the "new morality." Unfortunately, many fail to distinguish between external structure and dynamic function. Hatred and envy between brothers is about as bad for people today as it was for Cain and Abel. Bearing "false witness" or defrauding your neighbor does not work any better in the long run today than it did in Old Testament times. Whether it is Laban pawning off his second-class daughter on Jacob or a modern business swindle amidst dictating machines and computers, the two transactions are noteworthy for their similarities more than their differences. In either case someone's character was fractured (or ruptured) for such a breach of contract to be possible. You cannot break the contract (in this moral sense) without breaking the personal integrity, the backbone, of one or both of the parties to the contract.

Just because a new stress is being placed on the "intention" of relationships and behavior does not mean a lessening of the force or importance of morality in daily life in the new society. It means that morality is *more* than segments of external behavior. Jesus said that a person who hates his brother is heading in the direction of murder, and a man who "looks at a woman lustfully has already committed adultery with her in his heart" (Matt. 5:28). On the contrary, the Pharisees would have thought smugly to themselves, "Well, at least I didn't *do* anything about it." Jesus' dynamic and functional attitude toward morality took into account the intention, the direction toward which the person was moving. A sanctified intention, a loving and gracious disposition toward my neighbor, in short the kind of loving concern God has toward me, such an attitude is the prerequisite for ethical decisions. But unless the love and humane concern is in my heart, it will not really authentically influence my behavior. As long as I am merely acting out vicariously the will and wishes of parents, peers, society, and the policeman and the judge, my behavior may have all the appearances of being "good," but it is not essentially *moral*.

Many of us have never really had our moral fiber tested until we are alone with our decisions — so alone that even our loved ones will never know what our decisions have been. How will we act and what values will we hold fast to when we are not supported by family, friends, and personal connections, when we are alone in the crowd? Such a testing reveals whether we have a worthy character and sufficient backbone to stand straight as a man.

"There but for the Grace of God Go I"

The Christian is not arrogant and proud about any right decisions he might be able to make for several reasons. First, he knows of many times when he has not made the right decision, when his intentions and actions have been egocentric and divisive. He also remembers, when he sees someone else who has chosen the wrong path or has some conspicuous fault, the words of Jesus: "Judge not that you be not judged. . . . You hypocrite, first take the log out of your own eye, and then you will see clearly to take the speck out of your brother's eye." (Matt. 7:1-5)

Casting aside all judgmentalism (the harsh, negativistic kind to which Jesus referred) and simply doing the right thing for the sake of our neighbor and out of gratitude to God for all the blessings we have experienced, yes, that approach to morality is wonderfully freeing. Then it is a spontaneous joy to serve, to hold up one's end of the bargain of any contract, to be responsible. A person thus freed from social compulsion and the old "must" conscience of legalism does not dread the watchful eye of relatives and friends, nor does he find the temptations of a depersonalized environment or work situation overpowering. His internalized conscience, freed by grace, goes with him wherever he is; it strengthens him like a strong skeleton. It does not weigh him down like a burdensome suit of armor.

"Ah," you say, "but even strong men break their bones sometimes, especially if they are active." True indeed! Just so, the strong Christian knows that he is not above a fall now and then, a mistake, a misstep. He also knows that the same God who hopes he will do well is eager to raise him up, forgive him, heal his broken bones, and send him on his way again rehabilitated for the vocation that daily needs him. How wonderful such assurance is. Otherwise he might stay in bed all day in a fearful resolve not to break any bones. (Of course then he would waste away as an invalid.)

You see, the externals of life might change, but when it comes right down to essentials, many questions and issues are not so different basically from what they were "in the olden days."

PART III

HOW CAN I
LIVE ALL THE DAYS
OF MY LIFE?

Let us turn from diagnosis to action. We have discussed and analyzed some of the aspects of loneliness in our present age. Insight is not enough. We must know and decide what to do positively as our lives move forward into the future. Therefore, we turn from diagnosis to prognosis.

The collect for grace in the matins service has a wholesome forward thrust:

> O Lord, our heavenly Father, almighty and everlasting God, who hast safely brought us to the beginning of this day, defend us in the same with Thy mighty power and grant that this day we fall into no sin, neither run into any kind of danger; but *that all our doings, being ordered by Thy governance, may be righteous in Thy sight;* through Jesus Christ, Thy Son, our Lord, who liveth and reigneth with Thee and the Holy Ghost, ever one God, world without end. Amen.

The attitude here is: "It's a new day of grace; let's get at it." There is a sense of adventure in life, and why not? Jesus said: "I came that they may have life, and have it abundantly" (John 10:10). If the new day is a gift from God, it will be lived eagerly, gratefully, as a golden opportunity.

How can I live my life in such spirit that it continues to be a celebration, a worship? How can I keep from running down like a mechanical clock with its mainspring going slack. We want to think in organic terms: living, growing, changing, going from strength to strength — like our Lord, who "increased in wisdom and in stature and in favor with God and man."

CHAPTER 7

Creation Continues

Machines begin in good shape and gradually, relentlessly wear out. The cylinder in an auto engine, for example, begins its existence at a certain size. As the piston rubs against it through thousands of miles of driving, friction gradually wears down its sides even though perhaps not enough for the naked eye to see. But one thing is sure, it will not be able to restore itself to its original shape.

Living things have the capacity to grow and replenish their parts. If you burn yourself (moderately, of course), a blister develops as temporary protection. The dead skin finally peels off and you are as good as new underneath. Even healthy skin that is not damaged gradually sloughs off as new cells are laid down to take their turn. In short, creation continues as man lives.

Remaking and Reshaping Our Lives

Man is never a finished product; he is always in the process of becoming. If he chooses to exercise his full potential, he can have a great deal to say about what he becomes from day to day. In our day this is especially so. We are told that the average person today can expect to be involved in three distinct vocations, three different careers. How different this was from the former ideal in which a person settled down comfortably into a lifelong work and fairly predictable style of life.

It is by far easier to follow the famous old path of least resistance. For this reason many drift along aimlessly or float with the tide once their lifeboat is inflated. One such person was a lonely and unfulfilled clergyman who had not taken much responsibility for structuring his own life. At one point in our discussions he was shocked to realize, "I've never really made any significant decisions in my life. I drifted into marriage with my high school girl friend; my father-in-law chose my seminary and practically arranged for my first parish. It really isn't my life I'm living." Even the marriage distress he was in was not solved by his positive action; rather his wife was killed in a car accident. Finally he woke up, like a long-lost prodigal son, and "came to himself." His next career and his next marriage were creations for which he took responsibility — and what a difference it made in that man.

Note the persons, on the contrary, who do reshape and re-create their lives continually. They are the Albert Schweitzers (musician, theologian, physician); the inventors, finding something new about carbonized thread (Thomas Edison), trying out a piston-pipe contraption clamped onto the kitchen sink (Henry Ford); the creative people of all types — writers, scientists, innovators.

Lest we be tempted to think that such creative approach to life is found only among geniuses, let me share the warm and glowing example of an elderly tailor.

At 80 years of age he was virtually retired although people still pleaded with him to make just one more special suit for them. One day while I was making a pastoral call in his home, he shared with me the red thread of creativity that had run through his life. When he was first apprenticed as a tailor's helper in Denmark, he took his calling very seriously. He had just been confirmed, which meant that he was now considered a man, lived and boarded away from his parental home, wore long trousers, and was addressed formally by his last name. He leaned forward in his chair and said, "Pastor, before I put the shears to that first bolt of wool, I first prayed that God would guide me so that I would properly 'suit' the man who was to wear that garment. You see, God had been active in that material long before it came to me. He had helped the sheep to grow in the meadow, and the shepherds who cared for them. Then many men had tended the sometimes dangerous looms and knitting machines. And I was to be privileged to turn this cloth into a suit for someone to use for years."

Tailoring was really not a dull thing for this man. Every new day brought a new challenge. He was alert to creating something new every time he "put the shears to a bolt of wool." You will not be surprised to learn that this man was sought out by orthopedic surgeons in Boston who needed a tailor who would take special care in suiting an amputee, a man with curvature of the spine, a withered arm, and all manner of body disfigurement. You could trust your patient to such a tailor.

The cynic may say that such an attitude is not possible in a large automobile factory where routine and monotony of automation have sapped all the joy from work. Perhaps the day such an attitude is developed even in "trivial" things, the auto manufacturers will not need to recall hundreds of thousands of cars each year to correct an assortment of defects. Many is the lonely cynic who claims he cannot re-create or reshape either his life or his involvement in society and even nature. He just drifts aimlessly over the waterfall into the abyss of meaninglessness.

Destiny, Direction, and Discipline — In That Order

In a "personagraph" rating scale I ask counselees to indicate what their ultimate destiny is. What do they consider to be their real future? The most interesting aspect of their replies is the length or time span of what they mean by future destiny. Some just hope to get through to the weekend. Others have plans for their vacation months off. A mother may hope to live long enough to see her three children married and on their own. Some, thinking in terms of vocational destiny, dream of their retirement when they can finally do the many things for which they have saved money all their lives, the golden years when the pension program finally pays off. Occasionally a believer speaks in terms of "eternal life with God" as his ultimate destiny. Ask yourself frankly what your response would be if we had not already done some prompting in this paragraph.

Now that we have raised the question of what your attitude toward the future is, we can proceed to the next issue: What direction do you wish to take? Do you have a directional orientation? Do you know *where* you are headed and *why*? Or is the future just going to happen to you like a big surprise without your conscious involvement? Nothing makes one feel quite as lonely and helpless as that kind of aimlessness.

Some of us have never been very specific about the direction of our lives precisely because we have never committed ourselves to a goal with any real feeling of certainty. We have been tenuous, conditional, and hesitant when we have spoken about the future. Too often we have thought something was going to work out and then we had to go the rounds of relatives and friends explaining that we had changed our minds about the new job, the big trip, the house in the country, etc. Next time we'll play it safe and not tell anyone till it happens; that way there will be no undoing to do. Finally in discouragement we have said, "Why plan; it maybe won't work out anyway!"

Hold on! Perhaps there is another approach worth trying. Analyze what went wrong. Maybe the problem is announcing plans prematurely; or it could be lack of information and study before making the commitment. Consider the advice of Jesus concerning the cost of discipleship·

> Whoever does not bear his own cross and come after
> Me, cannot be My disciple. For which of you, desir-
> ing to build a tower, does not first sit down and count
> the cost, whether he has enough to complete it?
> Otherwise, when he has laid a foundation and is
> not able to finish, all who see it begin to mock him,
> saying, "This man began to build, and was not able
> to finish."

(Nothing makes one feel more lonely than being held up
to ridicule and being set "outside" the group.)

> So therefore, whoever of you does not renounce
> all that he has cannot be My disciple.
>
> (Luke 14:27-30, 33)

The problem could even be failure to trust the future
enough to follow through with a spontaneous and pioneer-
ing spirit. Moving into the future with a sense of direction
is too important an issue to forsake just because it hasn't
worked a few times in the past. Seek new directions if
necessary, but let them be thrusts into the future where
one's destiny lies beckoning.

Discipline for its own sake is largely a thing of the past;
for example, learning Latin just to develop the mind, or
studying historical dates just to train the memory. Today
people want a functional discipline, one that is practically
related to daily life. Since discipline originally meant
learning, we must ask what we mean by learning today and,
further, what learning in life means. Ideally learning is not
a mechanical process but a dynamic one in which the whole
person develops and grows along a certain line. The discipline that is involved in the continuous creation and re-
creation of our lives is what the church has referred to as
"growth in grace," increasingly learning what we are to

become, striving toward a godly destiny, remaining open to new insight and fresh inspiration. It is learning from each new day's experiences, trusting ourselves to be led by the Spirit into the future.

Spiritual Death Amidst Physical Life

In this day of striving after lengthened physical life by heroic means, transplants, and technology, we would do well to stop and consider the religious view of life and death. Spiritually speaking, physical death is not the worst thing that can happen to us. It would be more tragic to die spiritually amidst a strong and vigorous bodily health. Several references to such a contrast are found in Scripture:

> She who is a real widow and is left all alone has set her hope on God and continues in supplications and prayers night and day; whereas she who is self-indulgent is dead even while she lives.   (1 Tim. 5:5-7)

Or consider the words to the church in Sardis from The Revelation to John (3:1-2) "I know your works; you have the name of being alive, and you are dead. Awake, and strengthen what remains and is on the point of death."

In his Letter to the Ephesians St. Paul describes the condition of those who have followed the path of least resistance mentioned previously. Since they have followed the "course of this world" and not a godly destiny, they are already spiritually dead. Then whether they live 30 years or 80 years physically is of small consequence.

> And you He made alive, when you were dead through the trespasses and sins in which you once walked, following the course of this world, following the prince of the power of the air, the spirit that is now at work in the sons of disobedience.
>
> (Eph. 2:1-2)

And what of the hypocrites against whom Jesus lashed out? Their lives were as useful as dead men's bones within the whited sepulcher. (Matt. 23:27-28)

Yes, there is always the tragic possibility that you can end up dead on your feet, a walking zombie, a hollow shell. Spiritual life must be constantly regenerated, renewed, and revalidated. St. Paul found his inner life actually growing stronger while his physical life (buffeted by persecutions and hardships) was growing weaker. "So we do not lose heart. Though our outer nature is wasting away, our inner nature is being renewed every day." (2 Cor. 4:16)

Thus *creation continues.* If this is true of the tissues of the body, it is even more certain of the life of the spirit. Just because the spiritual life often seems less obvious and compelling, we must not be lulled into neglecting it. As the body needs diet and exercise, so the spiritual self needs a clear awareness of life's destiny with the commitment to values and God's purposes that give life meaning.

I find in Christianity that overarching and comprehensive faith that shows me my relationship to the universe of nature and to God, who is somehow behind it all; also my relationship to society both in its historical heritage and our contemporary era; and the significance of my own existence as a person who is sinful even while striving, yet loved by a gracious Father for Christ's sake.

The above testimony is what makes it possible for me to "live all the days of my life." No day may be perfect; but no day need be without meaning. My life has less chance of being basically lonely when I join my friend the Danish tailor in finding eternal significance even in my daily vocation. Family, friends, parties, golf, vacation, all these are bonuses and blessings, but they are as finite and fragile as I am myself. Thank heavens I don't have to count on a raise in pay (nice as it might be) to make life meaningful.

CHAPTER 8

Not Too Late to Change

If what we have said about the dynamic, growing nature of human personality is true, it is not only never too late to change, but change is inevitable and desirable. Remembering our "parable" in the Introduction, let us consider several implications of the change question.

Not to Change Is to Change

Since so many things about us are constantly changing, a strange but inevitable fact is this: Even if you stand still, your relationship to things about you changes. Take a simple example. You are standing absolutely still beside a road as a car approaches. Even though you remain motionless, your relationship to the car changes drastically. First you see only the windshield, headlights, and grille. A few moments later you see the side doors and windows as well as the two hubcaps on your side of the car. In a little while all you can see is the rear window, trunk, and taillights. Things would be quite different if you were moving at the same speed as the car, let us say in a car 100 feet behind it on the same highway. Your relationship to the car would remain the same and you would continually see only the back of the car, but neither its side nor front. It would also appear to be the same size.

Let us transpose this same process to personal relationships. Take a newly married couple with equal educational background. Yet the husband presses on learning new things in the business or professional world. He keeps up with the changes in political and economic thought, perhaps taking in-service training or night courses. His wife could busy herself with the kids and neighborhood gossip for the first 10 years of their marriage. The husband begins to look different to the wife as he roars away in the dust like the auto from our spectator in the preceding paragraph. For the wife to plead, "But I'm still the same gal you married," will only bring the husband's critical reply, "That's the trouble; times have changed. I've changed and you haven't; as a result we've drifted apart."

The same is true about the person who hopes not to change concerning etiquette, theological language and liturgical practices, family life, vocational patterns, lifestyles in society, fashions, and almost any other human institution or part of society you could mention

Nothing makes a person lonelier than being "left behind." And that is precisely what happens to persons who do not take the effort to "keep up with the times." They drift farther and farther from the mainstream of life, from the center of the action. Finally they are so far out on the periphery that their former associates forget to inquire about them; they drop out of the conscious awareness of other people, not because of the maliciousness of others but because of their own absence from the scene.

In case anyone thinks aging must rigidify and preclude change, he need only look at Jack Benny, his favorite busy aunt, or aged Simeon. Simeon was an old man, but he continued to look for a new thing (the consolation of Israel) and did not die till he saw it. And when he saw the baby Jesus, he was inspired to know that a lot of changes were in the offing: "Behold, this Child is set for the fall and rising of many in Israel." His eyes had seen "salvation," "a light for . . . Gentiles" and "glory to . . . Israel" (Luke 2:25-32). Here was an old man open to changing times.

Just think of the implications for change when we read in Rev. 21:5: "And He who sat upon the throne said, 'Behold, I make all things new.' "

Change is so dynamic a factor in family life that we see tragic results if one party is in the process of making some dramatic changes (recovering from alcoholism, faced with unemployment, or dying) and the rest of the family continues with a business-as-usual approach. No! In a healthy family changes in one member bring reciprocal reaction from others. It is like pulling on a tennis net. If one square changes, many other strands change their angles also. Jesus said it so well:

> Can the wedding guests mourn as long as the bridegroom is with them? The days will come, when the bridegroom is taken away from them, and then they will fast. And no one puts a piece of unshrunk cloth on an old garment, for the patch tears away from the garment, and a worse tear is made. Neither is new wine put into old wineskins; if it is, the skins burst, and the wine is spilled, and the skins are destroyed; but new wine is put into fresh wineskins, and so both are preserved.   (Matt. 9:15-17)

Change of Life and Change of Scene

Two men moved from the Midwest to New England to work. The first man found the change of scene invigorating. There were so many new sights, historic landmarks, the ocean with sandy beaches or rocky, wave-crashing shoreline, also new manners and mores, a difference in architecture, and much more. The second man found the people cold and unfriendly, the building styles outmoded, the cities drab, the gas lights old fashioned compared to his home town "where there was an electric light on every corner." In short, his new home and work situation came off very badly by comparison with how things were "back home." He was homesick and lonely, and no wonder he stayed only a short while on his job. His associates noted his sour attitude toward their community, region, and society. Obviously they were not drawn to him in any warm or personal way. Each reaped pretty much what was sown.

One should not assume that the moral of the above comparison is to pretend interest where there is none, or to hide all of one's true feelings for the sake of public relations. That type of phony front is seen through by others and really not appreciated. It is not likely to create confidence concerning one's integrity and honesty. Rather it's a matter of basic attitude—being open to new things, curious and interested; or being closed-minded, prejudiced, and exclusive about letting new experiences into one's life. A person can be curious about a new city, group, or theory without forsaking any of his own integrity or preferences; but at least he has been willing to be exposed to something that is not his own. He believes it is possible for things that are not his own to be of value too, even if he never possesses them himself as long as he lives.

The narrow person has a typical way of beginning any remark about the "other's" possessions or point of view or experience with "I just cannot understand how . . . ." Thus: "I just cannot understand how anyone would want to live in that town." ". . . do that kind of work all day." ". . . would hire a convict." ". . . would want to go there on vacation." Such a person truly cannot understand how it is possible to have an attitude or experience other than his own. The pity of it is that such a person cheats himself out of a great variety of viewpoints and shared experiences which would enrich his life and help him grow personally and spiritually. God is trying to enrich his life, but he is not willing to be open to such new opportunities whether it is a change of scene or any other kind of change.

Some rather harsh terms for such persons in Biblical language are "stiff-necked," "hardness of heart," "unrepentant," and "stubborn." Some well-known characters of the Bible record who were plagued with this attitude were the Pharaoh of Egypt with whom Moses dealt, Jonah, who resisted God's new assignment, and Jacob, who wrestled with the angel. Some came through and others not. If you find yourself stuck in a comfortable rut and fearful of change, it would not hurt to check your motivation. Let us hope it is for some good reason and not just resisting change for its own sake, or worse yet, an example of one of the spiritual disorders listed at the top of this paragraph.

Many Opportunities, but All Require Change

A person cannot benefit from a new opportunity, whether it be a new job, a new friendship, a new home, a new point of view, without undergoing more or less change. It is an adjustment to assimilate the new into what we now have. But it is so often well worth it. The new challenge brings out different aspects of our personality, new strengths and capacities we did not know we had before.

Going back to the heading of this section, "How Can I Live All the Days of My Life?" we will find a large part of the answer in the readiness to grasp new opportunities when they present themselves—or when we have created such opportunities. "It's a new day of grace; let's get at it!" Without a touch of adventure and search for the new, life becomes dull and monotonous, meaningless and often lonely. Staying in the same old spot while the rest of the world breezes by leaves one feeling isolated and cut off from the action.

The good news is that there are so often new ways of feeling and thinking even when we are not moving to new places or doing new things. There is the Danish tailor who found each new suit an opportunity to do something new (whereas many another tailor would have said he was doing "the same old thing day in and day out"). Each new day can be, and is if we but realize it, a day of grace and opportunity to experience what new thing God has in store for us.

CHAPTER 9

Look Outward

Lonely people are typically prone to brooding, self-oriented thoughts, introspection, moodiness. If such a person is approached by another, it is not long before the conversation is revolving around the concerns of this lonely person. The personal pronoun is prominently used— "I," "me," "mine," "my own," usually in the first person singular. There are few references to "you," "ours," "them," "others."

Such *turning inward* is characteristic of a whirlpool, which pulls everything into its center of gravity. The center and bottom of the whirlpool is the smallest point of focus. We use various tricks to focus attention on ourselves without appearing on the surface to do so because we know that basically it is considered bad manners. We send up little trial balloons and teasers. We bait our hook with tasty tidbits, and then when someone bites we say with apparent surprise, "Oh, hadn't you heard? Yes I had to go in for a checkup." A half hour later the conversation is still all about us and our symptoms. The difference between an attention seeker and a seeker after help is the fact that the former is not interested in help, advice, or any other constructive solution; the whole purpose of the conversation has been to be the focus of attention for a while. In a subtle way it is actually an attempt to be less lonely for a brief time, but it only alienates others because it is essentially parasitic. There is hardly ever that reciprocal interest

in the welfare and concerns of others, which is the response needed periodically to keep a true relationship
alive. So the whirlpool of egocentricity spins on relentlessly.

Looking outward out of genuine concern for others is
a broadening and enlarging experience. "It is more blessed
to give than to receive" in this case. Interest in others gen-
erates dialog instead of monolog. It lets others know we are
available for relationship not only as a dead-end receptacle.
Looking outward reminds us of the hustle and bustle of
life and of the interesting experiences of other people. It
fills our minds with new and different concerns, increases
our capacity for compassion, and lets others know we are
available to be of help, to be involved. In order that talk
about *people* not be limited to gossip, we need to add another dimension to the outward look.

What Is Important out There?

Talking about people can get petty, almost as petty as
talking about ourselves. The epitome is "Blondie" in the
comic strip chattering nonsense with the girls over the
phone. Often such talk degenerates to judgmental remarks about how good or bad, how out of date or avant-
garde so-and-so is.

We need to include discussion of issues, public policy,
social legislation, and values and priorities of our society.
These questions sharpen our objectivity and test our civic
concern in ways that personalized stories cannot do. We
may be driven to seek out the facts to back up our opinion,
to make a trip to the reference shelf of the public library,
to check our senator's voting record, to find out if the conditions are so bad as people say in neighboring nursing
homes. For the Christian all these issues are important because he has a social responsibility as his brother's keeper.

All the above-mentioned concerns and dozens more
which you could name in your community help to turn our

attention away from ourselves for a while and toward the needs of others. Such concern for what is going on "out there" in the real world also tends to get us involved, even committed. We find that we have common cause with others who are concerned about sex education in the schools, urban renewal, drug problems of youth, war, poverty, pollution, world missions, the plight of our favorite college, unemployment, Christian education, moral responsibility of the mass media, and a host of other issues of widespread influence. We could actually find ourselves having to be selective because it is a cinch we cannot make much of an impact by trying to cover the waterfront. But that is surely a much better predicament than having to sit around worrying which symptom you talked about last time to what few friends will still listen.

There are many exciting and important things going on "out there" in the real world; give yourself the benefit of being involved, and soon you will find that you are a benefit and blessing instead of a drag on society. And you will be less lonely to boot.

Recreation — A Godly Pursuit

In Genesis we read the first account of recreation and rest: "And on the seventh day God finished His work which He had done, and He *rested* on the seventh day from all His work which He had done. So God blessed the seventh day and hallowed it, because on it God rested from all His work which He had done in creation" (Gen. 2:2-3). Later this same principle is included as one of the Ten Commandments thus: "Remember the Sabbath day, to keep it holy. Six days you shall labor and do all your work; but the seventh day is a Sabbath to the Lord your God; in it you *shall not do any work*, you or your son or your daughter." (Ex. 20:8-10)

For some people life becomes dull, boring, monotonous,

and lonely because they do not heed this rhythm of work and rest, work and rest. This cycle is repeated in several ways. There is the recuperation of rest each night from each day's work. We also find in the cycle of nature's seasons a dormant and active alternation.

Sabbath rest today, of course, means something different from the nomadic days of Israel. The principle is that one must have a re-creation, a refreshing change from one's daily work and vocation. Thus the office man may spade up around his rose bushes, the sedentary worker play tennis, and the day laborer relax in front of the TV as he watches his favorite sport. Each must find that he needs to have his own kind of fun and "get away from the grind," as some say.

There must be change of pace as the Preacher says in Ecclesiastes:

> For everything there is a season, and a time
> for every matter under heaven: . . .
> a time to weep, and a time to laugh;
> a time to mourn, and a time to dance;
> a time to cast away stones, and a time
>   to gather stones together;
> a time to embrace, and a time to refrain
>   from embracing.   (Eccl. 3:1, 4-5)

Such change of pace is appropriate to each situation and develops the emotional and spiritual flexibility that everyone needs. It keeps us from getting into a rut. We need to be protected from painting the whole world with one color. There is nothing like a good "day off" to get us out of ourselves for a fresh look at what is "out there."

Humor

Gordon Allport, an eminent psychologist who appreciated the role of religion in mental health, claimed that humor and religion have much in common. Humor helps to get things back into perspective. When something really funny happens to a pompous old so-and-so, it sort of takes him down a peg and makes him join the human race again. When everyone at a meeting is taking himself too seriously, we appreciate the fellow who knows how to relieve the tension with a well-placed bit of humor. But this is humor in a constructive and wholesome sense, not the kind that is destructive and vicious, not the racist or pornographic jokes of which one is partially ashamed even in the telling. We think rather of the spontaneous humor that enlivens our spirits, that burst of laughter or smile that surprises us with its lightheartedness. There is that easily recognizable humor that is filled with joy and happiness. It has a contagion that makes everyone within its reach feel good.

In this sense Allport was right about a comparison between true humor and high religion. Religion also gives us a sense of perspective. It is hard to take oneself too seriously or pompously when in the Holy of Holies. All human foibles and pretensions are shown to be really ridiculous in the clear light of the majesty of God. How can man avoid smiling when he contemplates how his own little fussing and feuding must appear when set in the context of the Creator's eternity?

Finally

We are set in the midst of a great company of others who have had like experiences, worries, joys, loneliness, and fellowship as the writer to Hebrews declares so eloquently:

> Therefore, since we are surrounded by so great a cloud of witnesses, let us also lay aside every weight, and sin which clings so closely, and let us run with perseverance the race that is set before us,

looking to Jesus, the Pioneer and Perfector of our faith, who for the joy that was set before Him endured the cross, despising the shame, and is seated at the right hand of the throne of God.

(Heb. 12:1-2)

The believer, at any rate, does not need to look for company; he is already surrounded by a great company. At least for me it has been a great antidote against loneliness to be swept up in worship at matins to sing with others the majestic words of the *Te Deum Laudamus:*

The glorious company of the apostles praise Thee;
The goodly fellowship of the prophets praise Thee;
The noble army of martyrs praise Thee;
The holy church throughout all the world
   doth acknowledge Thee;
The Father of an infinite majesty;
Thine adorable true and only Son,
Also the Holy Ghost the Comforter.

Postscript: Where to Begin?

Begin where you are! Sound simple? It is not obvious to those who believe there is a better place and a better time to begin. Some want to wait till their circumstances change a bit for the better, others till they have sowed their wild oats, some till they have gotten certain affairs in order, others wish to wait till the present crisis or adjustment is past; then they will "begin living."

God accepts you as you are; so can you, without conditions and qualifications, without waiting for improvement or insight. That is the *good news* otherwise known as the Gospel. You do not even need to wait till you have earned it; accept new life now as a gift. By faith and in communion with other believers you can have victory over loneliness and isolation, shame and guilt, sickness and death. It is a gift of grace. Grace knows neither time nor geography; therefore, there is no better time to begin living than now nor a better place than exactly where you are sitting.

What has been set forth in this little book is nothing new; essentially it is a very old story. We have merely tried to reask some of the old questions in the setting of our modern day. In a very real sense the cure for loneliness has always been the same.

Check List of Some Helpful Resources

Persons can be a great help when things are getting us down. The following types of persons are just a few reminders that you need not face problems all alone. Give one or several a try until you get the help you need. But please approach them with an open mind and a hopeful attitude.

Relatives

Don't cross them all off your list till you have given them a chance; if not your mother maybe a cousin or uncle.

Friends

They may be more understanding than you think.

Pastor

He has helped many others before you, and it is not imposing because it is part of his calling.

Hospital Chaplain

Some pastors specialize in pastoral care and counseling and devote most of their time to it

Social Worker

A trained person who will listen with understanding and has many resources at her fingertips.

Counselor

Some specialize in vocational guidance, others in personality problems. They work in schools, hospitals, and agencies of many kinds.

Physician

Sometimes a physical examination reveals some disorder or imbalance which can adversely influence your personality adjustment and ability to get along with people or work effectively at your job. An old Latin motto reads: "A healthy mind in a healthy body."

Psychiatrist

He can help with problems of mental illness and has access to hospitalization and medical facilities. If your family physician refers you to him, use him as a welcome source of help.

Agencies and institutions have been especially created just to be available to help the hundreds of people who turn to them for service. It would be a pity if you or anyone you know should go without the help needed while these fine services go unused.

Parish Church

Yes, congregations have many subgroups of support, guidance, education, and fellowship as well as their total ministry in time of sickness, bereavement, crisis, and regular worship.

Travelers' Aid

Usually a desk or booth may be found in any large depot or terminal where the stranger can be helped over a rough spot.

Salvation Army

Transients and the down-and-out have found a safe harbor, temporary lodging, and material aid while trying for a second chance.

Lutheran Social Service (or Welfare Agency)

One of many denominational social service resources helping unmarried parents, arranging adoptions, doing family counseling, providing chaplaincy and counseling services of various kinds. (Catholic Charities a counterpart)

County Welfare Department

Aid is given to those on relief, old-age assistance, to the blind and otherwise handicapped, those in need of medical care, those seeking employment, needing housing, etc. (Often in the county court house; in larger cities also check city hall)

Community Mental Health Center

No one is very far from such an outpatient counseling center which helps people with a variety of problems. Group therapy is often part of their program.

Alcoholics Anonymous
One of the many types of self-help groups dealing with persons who all have the same basic type of problem. Other groups are concerned about drug addicts, "parents without partners," colostomy patients, parolees, etc.

Associations for the Mentally Retarded (and other problems)
A gathering of parents and others having to deal with a common problem, often one that sets them apart and makes them lonely without the company of others facing the same situation.

Recreation Centers
A place for hobbies, sports, folk dancing, meeting new people — the community's parlor.

Educational Opportunities
Adult and night classes at the local high school or community college, lectures, concerts, plays, museums, libraries, and other cultural resources.